A Kangaroo Grows Up

by Amanda Doering Tourville

illustrated by Michael Denman and William J. Huiett

Special thanks to our advisers for their expertise:

Zoological Society of San Diego
San Diego Zoo
San Diego, California

Susan Kesselring, M.A., Literacy Educator
Rosemount–Apple Valley–Eagan (Minnesota) School District

Editor: Christianne Jones
Designers: Angela Kilmer and Abbey Fitzgerald
Page Production: Melissa Kes
Art Director: Nathan Gassman
The illustrations in this book were created with acrylics.

Picture Window Books
5115 Excelsior Boulevard, Suite 232
Minneapolis, MN 55416
877-845-8392
www.picturewindowbooks.com

Printed in the United States of America.

Library of Congress Cataloging-in-Publication Data
Doering Tourville, Amanda, 1980-
A kangaroo grows up / by Amanda Doering Tourville ;
Illustrated by Michael Denman & William J. Huiett.
p. cm. — (Wild animals)
Includes bibliographical references and index.
ISBN-13: 978-1-4048-3160-5 (library binding)
ISBN-10: 1-4048-3160-6 (library binding)
ISBN-13: 987-1-4048-3569-6 (paperback)
ISBN-10: 1-4048-3569-5 (paperback)
1. Kangaroos—Infancy—Juvenile literature. 2. Kangaroos—Development—Juvenile
literature. I. Denman, Michael, ill. II. Huiett, William J., 1943- ill. III. Title.
QL737.M35D63 2007
599.2'22139—dc22   2006027308

Welcome to the world of wild animals! Follow a baby kangaroo as he grows up in Australia. Watch as he grows from a tiny joey into a strong, fast kangaroo.

A new kangaroo is born in Australia.
The tiny joey is pink, hairless, and blind.
He drinks milk from his mother.

A joey uses its sense of smell to crawl
through the mother's fur and find its
warm pouch.

4

Every so often, another kangaroo's head pops into the pouch. This is the joey's big sister. She also drinks milk from her mother.

A group of kangaroos is called a mob.

6

The new joey is hidden and safe inside his mother's pouch. He will stay their for the next six months, drinking milk and getting bigger and stronger.

At six months old, the joey peeks his head out of the pouch. For the first time, he sees the outside world. He sees other kangaroos, too. Some kangaroos are resting in the early morning light. Others are eating grass and plants.

Kangaroos are nocturnal. They are active late in the evening or at night. They rest during the day.

A few days later, the joey crawls out of his mother's pouch and falls to the ground. He picks himself up, and his mother licks him clean. He now weighs about 7 pounds (3 kilograms).

The joey tries out his legs and begins to hop for the first time. Over the next month, he spends more and more time outside his mother's pouch. His legs get stronger, and he can hop longer.

When a joey jumps into its mother's pouch, it completes a full somersault inside the pouch and ends up facing out.

11

The joey spots an animal he's never seen before. It is a wild dingo. He quickly hops back into his mother's pouch, where he is safe.

Most full-grown kangaroos don't have any natural enemies, but wild dogs, called dingos, and large eagles sometimes catch and eat small joeys.

Female kangaroos have strong muscles that control their pouch. They can loosen their muscles to let a joey in, or they can squeeze their muscles to close their pouch.

14

One day, the joey tries to crawl into his mother's pouch. Oh, no! He can't get in! His mother has tightened the strong muscles in her pouch so that the joey can't enter. This is her way of telling her baby that he's old enough to live outside of her pouch.

The joey is now eight months old. He still drinks milk from his mother, but he's beginning to eat grasses and other plants.

One day, the joey pops his head into his mother's pouch to feed. He sees a tiny joey drinking milk. This new joey is his little brother.

Female kangaroos are almost always pregnant. As soon as one joey is fully out of the pouch, a new joey is born.

Now one year old, the joey no longer needs his mother's milk. He eats other plants like the older kangaroos.

Kangaroos can go without water for long periods of time. They get the water they need from the green plants and grasses they eat.

The joey remains close to his mother, but he plays with other joeys his age. The young kangaroos play-fight by boxing and kicking one another.

Adult kangaroos may weigh 200 pounds (90 kg) and can be 6 feet (1.8 meters) tall.

Over the next few years, the joey grows stronger and becomes more independent. At five years old, he weighs 115 pounds (52 kg). He will continue to grow for the rest of his life.

It is time for the young kangaroo to leave the mob. He hops off to find a mate and start a family of his own.

Kangaroo Diagram

① **EYES** Kangaroos can't see very well up close, but they can spot predators from far away.

② **POUCH** Female kangaroos have a pouch to keep their young safe and warm.

③ **LEGS** Kangaroos can't walk. They use their strong legs to hop.

④ **FEET** Kangaroos hop by pushing off from their long feet.

⑤ **TAIL** Kangaroos have long, thick tails that help them balance when they hop.

Map

There are many different kinds of kangaroos. The kangaroos in this book are red kangaroos. They live in Australia.

Glossary

boxing—attacking and protecting using the fists; kangaroos box each other with their paws to win mates

dingo—a wild Australian dog

independent—not relying on something or someone else

joey—a baby kangaroo

mate—a male or female with which to produce young

mob—a large group of kangaroos

predators—an animal that hunts and eats other animals

To Learn More

At the Library

Eckart, Edana. *Red Kangaroo*. New York: Children's Press, 2003.
Hewett, Joan. *A Kangaroo Joey Grows Up*. Minneapolis: Carolrhoda Books, 2002.
Spilsbury, Richard and Louise. *A Mob of Kangaroos*. Chicago: Heinemann Library, 2004.

On the Web

FactHound offers a safe, fun way to find Web sites related to this book. All of the sites on FactHound have been researched by our staff.

1. Visit *www.facthound.com*
2. Type in this special code: 1404831606
3. Click on the FETCH IT button.

Your trusty FactHound will fetch the best sites for you!

Index

Look for all of the books in the Wild Animals series:

A Baboon Grows Up

A Crocodile Grows Up

An Elephant Grows Up

A Giraffe Grows Up

A Hippopotamus Grows Up

A Jaguar Grows Up

A Kangaroo Grows Up

A Lion Grows Up

A Rhinoceros Grows Up

A Tiger Grows Up